Roots & Relationships:
Fostering Real Connections Beyond the Virtual

George Wu

Roots & Relationships: Fostering Real Connections Beyond the Virtual

Published by Plantingle LLC (plantingle@gmail.com)

ISBN 979-8-9884941-1-9 (paperback)
ISBN 979-8-9884941-2-6 (e-book)

Contents

CHAPTER ONE

The Offline Oasis

In today's hyper-connected world, digital technology permeates nearly every aspect of our lives, fundamentally altering how we communicate and connect. From social media platforms to messaging apps, screens have become the primary interface through which we engage in conversations and relationships. While this digital revolution has undeniably brought unprecedented convenience and connectivity, it has also ushered in a profound shift in our interactions, raising crucial questions about the authenticity and depth of our relationships.

At the heart of this transformation lies a critical crossroads: the intersection between the virtual and the tangible, where the allure of digital connections clashes with the enduring value of face-to-face communication. This juncture represents far more than a mere technological advancement; it symbolizes a pivotal moment in human interaction, where the very essence of genuine connection hangs in the balance.

At the crossroads mentioned in the paragraph, imagine two paths diverging: one leads to deeper, meaningful face-to-face interactions, while the other continues down the path of digital dominance, where screens mediate our relationships. For example, consider a scenario where a group of friends gathers for dinner. On the one hand, they could engage in lively, in-person conversations, sharing stories with laughter and creating cherished memories. On the other hand, they might spend the evening glued to their phones, scrolling through social media feeds, only intermittently glancing up to acknowledge each other. This junction represents the choice between nurturing authentic connections or succumbing to the allure of digital distractions.

As we navigate this evolving landscape, it becomes increasingly evident that the authenticity of face-to-face relationships stands at a crossroads. On one path lies the allure of digital convenience, where screens mediate our interactions, offering instant gratification and seemingly endless possibilities for connection. Yet, amidst this digital frenzy, a growing sense of disconnection exists—a longing for the tangible warmth of human presence, the spontaneity of unscripted conversations, and the intimacy of shared experiences.

On the other path lies the enduring value of face-to-face communication—the timeless art of truly being present with one another. Genuine connection flourishes in the absence of screens and the distractions they entail. In the simple act of meeting eye-to-eye, sharing laughter, and engaging in meaningful dialogue, we reaffirm the irreplaceable richness of human connection.

In the following chapters, we will explore this dichotomy between the real and virtual, along with the complexities of digital communication and its impact on the authenticity of our relationships. Through insightful observations, thought-provoking anecdotes, and practical strategies, we will uncover the challenges and opportunities in reconciling digital convenience and the enduring essence of face-to-face connection.

Humankind recently experienced the stress of being isolated when the epidemic unfolded into a pandemic with the spread of COVID-19. It is now a palpable fear for many that another pandemic with its physically isolating regulations may occur. Therefore, having weathered the mental and physical toll, there is a craving for social offline connections. Perceiving this need, I created a group that grew beyond my imagination.

I initially created this group because the Bay Area in Silicon Valley appeared bland as everything closed early, and people needed to dress better or value their appearances more. I could not see myself living and working here in a non-stimulated environment. Almost everyone in the Bay Area who is in tech has a lot of money but only a little life experience. The traditional age of most people within the Bay Area is about ten years behind that of other cities. Even at work, I am amazed when Vice Presidents at my company start throwing tantrums like kids. I told myself I did not want to become like that. So, I started a group mainly to maintain my language skills and have an engaging social life where I will not become a typical Bay Area resident who is money-rich but life-poor.

I also understand how hard it is to create a group and community when people first start, so I decided to share as much as I know from my experience so that others who start a similar group will enjoy the process and shortcut all the hardships that I have gone through. I detail what I learned in this book to help others build similar communities.

The Digital Paradox and Online Platforms

In the age of unparalleled connectivity, our fingertips glide across screens, forming friendships and alliances in the vast landscape of cyberspace. Yet, within this digital tapestry, a peculiar paradox unfolds. The more we connect online, the more we crave authentic, tangible connections offline. How often have we felt that the vibe from the online community is just different from that of an offline community? Why do we yearn for more physical, face-to-face connections in an era of unprecedented digital connectivity? The online world was never supposed to replace the offline world; it was supposed to be a better bridge between people. Our social interactions and reactions are vital and potent; when we experience social pain—a snub, a cruel word—the feeling is as accurate as physical pain. In his new book entitled Social: Why Our Brains Are Wired to Connect, Matthew Lieberman also makes a case that our need to connect is as fundamental as our need for food and water. Taking this conversation forward, this section will explore the psychology behind our innate need for genuine human interactions and position various online platforms, from Discord to Meetup.com, as a guiding light, leading us back to the roots of community building. It is time to use what is Online to build back the Offline communities.

Although the later generations are looking for more and more virtual experiences, think of virtual dancing parties as an example. The social nuances of in-person meetings are lost in that environment. With convenience comes a need for more intimacy. For instance, Kuzminykh and Rintel (2020b) found participants reported feeling lower motivation to engage both behaviorally and cognitively when participating in a meeting remotely versus face to face. So, you see, there is a need for offline communities; it brings out our innate need for connection.

Online platforms are incredible technological feats that have made seamless connections possible. However, in the last two decades, people have increasingly preferred digital over physical connections, and our innate craving for physical human connection has been exposed. Human connection is the very fabric that binds us together, creating empathy, understanding, and belonging patterns. At its core, it transcends mere proximity or technological intermediaries; it encompasses the profound exchange of emotions, thoughts, and experiences when individuals come together in physical space. Offline social connection offers unparalleled depth and richness in the digital realm. In face-to-face interactions, we share words and subtle cues—facial expressions, gestures, and tones of voice—that convey nuance and depth of meaning. These nonverbal signals serve as vital conduits for empathy and understanding, fostering a sense of closeness and mutual resonance essential for our emotional well-being.

Moreover, offline social connection protects users from the constant bombardment of digital stimuli, offering a space for genuine presence and authentic engagement. In a world increasingly dominated by screens and virtual encounters, nurturing offline social connections becomes a source of solace and a vital lifeline to our shared humanity. Through these tangible, face-to-face interactions, we find solace, support, and a profound sense of belonging—a reminder that, despite the allure of digital convenience, our deepest fulfillment ultimately lies in the warmth of human connection.

Despite our continuing woes stemming from a lack of physical connections and the insecurities we have harbored from spending too long behind screens, we, as social animals, can find a way out. Online platforms can be a bridge to bring people closer to the real world.

This book guides you in leveraging various platforms and tools to help facilitate that interaction. It will also use the group I created through Meetup.com as an example of cultivating thriving offline communities. You can use platforms like Facebook groups, Craigslist, Excel spreadsheets, and messaging groups (WhatsApp, Kakao, Line, Discord, etc.) to replace Meetup.com.

Setting the Stage

Before diving into community leadership's intricacies, let us set the stage. Envision a lively café where laughter mingles with the aroma of coffee, a park where diverse individuals converge for a shared passion, or a snug library hosting discussions that transcend the pages of books. We will revisit these scenes as we explore the art of fostering offline connections.

The Crux of Connection

The connection lies at the heart of our human experience. As we embark on this journey, let us peel back the digital noise layers and rediscover the joy, richness, and authenticity. Join me as we unravel the potential within to create meaningful, lasting communities beyond the confines of the virtual world.

The first steps into the offline oasis are yours. In the following pages, we will delve into the offline community landscape, unraveling its nuances and potential. The adventure promises insights, inspiration, and practical strategies to weave a tapestry of vibrant offline communities. Your journey begins here.

Note to the Reader: This book is not merely a guide; it is an invitation to become a curator of connections, a steward of genuine human bonds. Whether you are a seasoned community leader or a newcomer stepping into the world of community building, these pages offer a roadmap to create, nurture, and cherish the offline oasis awaiting you.

CHAPTER TWO

Understanding the Offline Community Landscape

In learning to create an offline community, we will use Meetup.com as an example because that is where I made my group. However, using other platforms like social media, such as a Facebook group, is also okay; it is essential to understand the landscape that shapes this dynamic platform. You can easily reference Facebook or Messenger groups with 500 members, etc. I am using Meetup.com as an example, but you can easily insert Meetup into any of the formats mentioned before.

Like others, offline community-unveiled social platforms such as Meetup.com are virtual town squares where communities gather, connect, and grow. Understanding its architecture, features, and functionalities is like unlocking the door to a realm of possibilities.

The Anatomy of Offline Community

The offline community thrives on diversity, with groups spanning an array of interests, from tech enthusiasts and book lovers to hiking fans. This section explores the significance of selecting the right category and keywords, ensuring your group finds its niche amid the vast offline community space in whatever platform you choose. Picking the right group and categories is essential. Also, it pays to be as granular as possible instead of a one-size catch-all.

For example, picking "Art" or "Business" is not detailed enough. Selecting things such as "art walks" and "fundraising" to narrow the scope is better. The more precise you are with your intention, the better others will understand what you stand for. Sure, you can only catch some of them in your community. Still, you want to avoid a big community for an offline community anyway. Imagine trying to find venues for 100 people all the time. So, it is best to stay very niche-specific.

Member Profiles and Networking

Its members are central to the experience of forming communities. In this section, we'll unravel the intricacies of member profiles, emphasizing the importance of networking within and beyond your community. Building connections within the platform lays the foundation for fostering offline connections. There are a few options for thinking of member profiles and networking.

1. Keep it as private and general as possible to avoid sharing your information.

2. Share as much information as possible to generate a connection.

3. Share what you are comfortable with.

Here are three suggestions for improving your profiles. Instead of spending excessive time on them (a hint to Facebook users), focus on the basics. A headshot, so people know who you are, and then a few things you can put in to get the profile started. As you join groups, you notice the information other members fill in. Next, what you want to do is the following steps:

1. Search the top five to ten active member profiles in your joined groups.

2. Look through what details they share that are common across all. Fill in the details that mimic those details (if you already have more information, you can skip this step).

3. Rinse and repeat the top two steps with the new groups you join.

In this scenario, your member profile is almost guaranteed to align with whichever group you associate with. Aligning your profile with the group saves you time in two factors: (1) figuring out how much is too much and how little is too little. And (2) help you quickly get onboarded to the platform so that you do not come across as a beginner or a serial killer who tries to hide all this information.

Analyzing Successful Groups

Do Your Research

To comprehend the landscape fully, we dissect successful groups' anatomy. One of the best ways to see what successful groups do is to attend a variety that interests you and see what works and does not with each group. A couple of things to keep in mind:

1. The group's attitude in general:

    a. Do they care if you are a few minutes late?

    b. Is there a strict rule adherence policy?

        i. For example, you are out of the group if there are three no-shows.

    c. Is it a free-form or structured event with a clear agenda?

2. People who get drawn to the group:

a. Do they all have certain things in common that tie the group together? If so, what is that? If not, why not?

b. Are there consistent regulars who come to the event, or are new people constantly coming (you want to see repeat attendees; otherwise, the event could be more sustainable)?

3. What is sustaining the group?

a. For example, are the organizers funding all the activities? Are they collecting memberships? Are they getting sponsored by companies?

b. There has to be a time and funding source that keeps the group going, or it will eventually disband or become unpleasant.

Identifying Your Target Audience

After learning from attending different groups and events, identifying your target audience is a pivotal step in building communities. By understanding the demographics and interests of potential members, you can tailor your group to meet their needs, ensuring a higher likelihood of engagement and sustained growth. You want to do some exercise on how you would enjoy the event. The event should be fun, but you should not start it if it is similar to a suffocating job. So, identify people most similar to you and what kind of event you wish to entail. Use the above questions to tailor a matrix to what matters most to you.

1. Event size

2. Location

3. Rules or regulations

4. Type of people and personalities

5. Others

Using those criteria, make sure to check that you would attend the event at the end because, after all, you did it for yourself. If you did not, then why bother? You can make way more money by investing in doing your day job better than trying to make money from your created group.

Niche and Differentiation

Finding your niche is critical to standing out in the vast expanse of groups. We delve into the art of differentiation, examining how successful groups carve their space within broader categories. Your ability to define a unique and compelling group identity will be crucial in attracting and retaining members.

It is essential to be as narrow as possible instead of trying to catch a wide net. For example, I would like to build on the previous example in my group. I have many different interests listed below:

1. Alcohol

2. Scuba Diving

3. ATVing

4. Tennis

5. Boardgames

6. Travel

7. Dating

8. Stocks

9. Cryptocurrency

10. Business

11. Languages

12. Others

As you can see, my list is long. Having one group that fulfills all your desires and needs takes time and effort. Imagine one event where you have five people with different interests. That means you have to be the one to talk to everyone, and they do not want to talk to each other (I am exaggerating here, but you get the point). Instead, make it so narrow and focused on things you enjoy. My current Meetup group was centered on the Korean language. I could have chosen K-pop or K-drama, which has the most fan base. But I have absolutely ZERO interest in talking about K-pop or K-drama for the entire event. I would be bored out of my mind. So, I expanded to the Korean language, which can use K-pop or K-drama as a subcategory to enhance Korean language learning. I am okay with spending the entire session practicing my Korean.

My purpose is that by being as niche as possible, you guarantee that everyone who comes to your event has a central anchor that ties them together. The reason most religious groups get together is the beliefs and values that bind them together. Similarly, those countries have the inherent culture that binds them together. You need an anchor to have people bind to that group. With an anchor, it is easy. As the group expands, the anchor that binds them will become weaker and weaker due to its size, so it is essential to have that anchor as strong as possible in the beginning.

Crafting an Engaging Page

Your front landing page is your group's digital storefront. From selecting an eye-catching group name to designing an attractive logo, every element contributes to your group's first impression of potential members.

When you are first starting, it is hard, so keep it general and try to get people from other social circles to join your group regularly to establish some cadence. However, take pictures and show how many people attend your event. The more people participate with many images of human heads and faces, the better it is. It is creating credibility. Also, if you have a few members, to begin with, find some physically attractive friends and pose pictures to get the desirable marketing you need. Think of it as sales and dating; you want to have at least them give you a chance for a first meeting or date; otherwise, no matter how awesome you structure the event, no one experiencing it will make any difference. So having people attend is more important than having a perfect first event. After all, you can always learn and tell people that you just started the group. It will have people give you some slack, to be honest.

In terms of descriptions, similarly, the more detail you have, the better it is. Also, beyond just the detail, make sure the vibe checks out. People will think this is a professional or educational group if the descriptions are formal. In contrast, if your descriptions are very casual regarding vibe, people will mostly associate them with a hobby or social group focusing on your chosen theme.

Crafting an engaging landing page is essential to drawing in and retaining visitors. It utilizes compelling visuals, clear calls to action, and intuitive navigation to create a seamless and captivating user experience. However, the art of engagement is wider than the digital world. Equally important is fostering positive interactions and relationships in offline communities. Just as thoughtful design and user-focused strategies are vital online, practicing etiquette and best practices in face-to-face interactions can build strong, supportive community networks.

Etiquette and Best Practices

Group Descriptions and Expectations

Navigating the landscape requires adherence to certain etiquettes and best practices. We explore the art of crafting compelling group descriptions and setting clear expectations for members. Clarity in communication sets the stage for a positive and cohesive community experience.

Frankly, if you do not know how to establish boundaries, you should seek a therapist or learn from a coach and set them correctly. Otherwise, partner with someone who can. You will run into various encounters, from arguing with the venue staff to even your attendees. The events will fall apart if you do not have a solid and clear boundary between tolerable and not. Not because your intention could be better but because starting any group requires a strong foundation. Like before, we mentioned an anchor regarding the theme; the initial members also need to be the anchor to setting clear boundaries, either explicitly or implicitly.

Case Study:

In one of the other Meetups from Meetup.com that I was part of, the Meetup group increased from ten people to a hundred in a few months from organic word of mouth. It then crashed and burned at the six-month mark. What happened was that the organizers started to fight among themselves and then later banded together and created a new group, took all the members to the new group, and ostracized the founder from joining that group. The reason was that the founder did not have a clear boundary in establishing acceptable and unacceptable behavior in the group.

One of the members wanted to be an organizer to help out, and then more members started to volunteer, and the group started to get big. However, one of the organizers began to remove members simply because he did not like that person for whatever reason. The founder did not step in and say that it was not acceptable or remove the organizers' privileges. What happened was that toxic behavior continued when he started to remove other organizers from the group when he had a bad experience with them. So now, the members are unhappy, and the organizers are not happy either.

Guess what happened?

They all started to turn to the founder to settle the dispute. The founder decided to remove all organizers and start new rules inconsistent with what had been implicitly stated. Initially, it was a loose meetup where people hung out and went as they pleased. Suddenly, he implemented harsh conditions on those who showed up late, including no-shows and organizer criteria, among other such a drastic culture change in the Meetup group that there was a lot of chaos, him from a "nice" guy to becoming a "dictator" because he could not establish a clear boundary on what was acceptable and what was not and wanted to please everyone in the beginning. As time progressed, the Meetup eventually fell apart within six months.

As a result, it is essential to establish certain boundaries and let people know what is acceptable and what is not acceptable behavior. There are generally two ways to go about this.

1. Clearly stated rules and regulations that people will follow and know there will be no exceptions.

2. Behavior management involves giving fewer privileges to those who disrupt and more privileges to those who enhance the group.

The first way is much easier because everything is documented so that you can follow the process. The con is that it is easier to make exceptions when people feel they are not treated fairly.

The second is my preferred way, as you are not forcing anyone to do anything. They can choose to do whatever they want, but if they do the stuff you hope they do, they are ranked at the bottom of priority compared to the rest of the members. So they are, in effect, incentivized not to do that. The con is that this takes time to execute. It is easier to execute with some background in user experience design, psychology, or other similar user-related educational or professional/personal experience. I even find myself needing help with how to execute it effectively. However, one of the principles I learned from Buddhism was the concept of cause and effect. That teaching mentioned not judging behavior but treating it as a business transaction. Am

I okay with the potential consequence of my behavior? If so, execute.

Similarly, telling members this is what I plan to do; you do not have to agree to it, but this is what I am going to do, and you are welcome to abide or not abide; for new founders, I highly recommend the first approach and the start of the second approach later. I only started with the second approach because of my professional and volunteering experiences, ranging from being a school teacher, product management, user experience, and hanging out with my friends from the entertainment industry. With that experience, executing the second option would be easier for me. It is still very tough for me at the moment. So, weigh your options and manage accordingly.

Setting Up for Success

Scheduling and Consistency

A well-thought-out schedule is the backbone of successful event groups. I want to emphasize the importance of consistency. A regular and predictable event schedule fosters member engagement and builds a sense of community continuity. Again, leveraging my professional experience in user design, having a consistent schedule creates a habit for the members.

When the members develop a habit, showing up and putting it on their calendar becomes second nature to them. Many people fear uncertainty. By making events at the same time on a regular cadence, people will naturally integrate this group into the normalcy of their lives.

Incorporating Social Elements

Beyond the events, successful groups understand the significance of social elements. Whether pre-event networking, post-event discussions, or shared online spaces, incorporating social components enhances the overall community experience.

There are many ways to go about this, from creating unofficial events from the event by having drinks and dinners, among other things. Additionally, keep the program on the agenda and talk about personal things to get a personal connection and relationship in the future.

Summary

As we conclude this chapter, we have embarked on a journey through the offline community landscape. Understanding the platform's architecture, analyzing successful groups, and honing in on your target audience are crucial steps in establishing a thriving community. The following chapters will build upon this foundation, guiding you in the practical application of these insights.

CHAPTER THREE

Planning and Launching Your Offline Group

Creating a group is more than a digital endeavor—crafting a community with a purpose. This chapter will delve deeper into the strategic planning required to give life to your vision. From defining your group's identity to setting up an inviting marketing, each step is crucial in creating a foundation for a thriving community.

Defining Your Group's Purpose and Goals

A well-defined purpose and clear goals provide a strong foundation for your group. This clarity ensures that all activities and decisions align with your core mission, creating a cohesive and focused community. By clearly articulating your group's mission and goals, you attract individuals who share your vision and are genuinely interested in your group's offerings. This alignment leads to a more engaged and committed membership base. Let us see how you can do that.

Crafting a Mission Statement

A mission statement is the compass that guides your group. It distills your community's essence into a few sentences, offering clarity to potential members and yourself. Work through a series of exercises to precisely articulate your group's mission, capturing the spirit that will attract like-minded individuals.

You can Google various companies' mission statements, such as Apple's, "bringing the best user experience to customers through innovative hardware, software, and services."

Other approaches include brainstorming: If you were never around, what would you want the group you created to be known as? Here are different ideas that will help you brainstorm the mission statement for the group you are creating.

1. What one thing do I want everyone to take away from this group?

2. What people would like to know about my group?

3. What kind of people do I want in my group?

4. What age range do I want my group to consist of?

5. What type of activities do I want my group to have?

6. What do I want to say about my group if I can talk about it on TV?

Notice how all the questions centered around "what" and nothing else. Here were my answers when I started the group.

1. I want everybody to feel content and safe when interacting with my group

2. I want people to know that this is a reliable group

3. I want people who would be down to do things last minute

4. I want it to have no age range

5. I want my group to have a lot of drinking parties

6. N/A

As you can see, my answers were vague when I started the group. They did not quite have a direction, but still highlighted a few key things I wanted to include: (1) Safety, (2) Relatedness, and (3) Spontaneous Fun.

Knowing a few fundamental values you want to embed in the group will already be on your way to establishing an anchor for longevity for your group.

As the group matured after a year, I answered these questions differently.

1. Make one close friend from the group

2. It is a privilege to be part of this group

3. People who support each other

4. Geared toward people without toddlers

5. Variety of events

6. It is a fun, social way to practice your Korean skills

As you can see, as my group grew, my answer also started to change. We do not have to stick to what we have already established as time changes. You can evolve the group's answers over time. However, the three things that stayed with the group were (1) Safety, (2) Relatedness, and (3) Spontaneous Fun; so you see, the original values never disappeared. Even though the answer had changed, the core thing that created the group remained. Those core attributes are best left intact.

Identifying Core Themes and Interests

Dive deep into the passions that fuel your community. Through exercises and reflection, pinpoint the core themes and interests that will define your group. These insights will guide your initial content and events and attract members who resonate with your group's essence.

As mentioned in the previous sections, identifying those core attributes will also help you identify core themes and interests. In my example, I chose the Korean language to create a fun, spontaneous environment. That means when I first started, I would choose a different location every single time so that the event would always be fresh and spontaneous. However, I did have one common theme: it is at a cafe. The cafe part is essential as every location will be a cafe/coffee house/tea house so that people can get an idea of what kind of venue it is so there is an air of familiarity. Similarly, based on your core principles for your event or group, the type of event surrounding location, environment, or ambiance you want to create will significantly impact establishing a "familiarity" anchor that people can reasonably predict in the coming events.

Crafting a Compelling Group Description

Your group's description is your virtual handshake—a critical first impression. Learn the art of storytelling to create a description that informs and captivates. We will explore techniques to infuse personality, enthusiasm, and clarity, making your group irresistible to potential members.

You can use many frameworks to create a compelling story instead of a wide array of frameworks that will confuse you and prevent you from taking action through analysis paralysis.

Here is a three-step framework that you can adopt to move ahead:

1. Invoke emotions through connections

2. Create a background story

3. Actions you want the audience to take:

I read that you can think of the IRS (so now you can remember it, especially if you pay taxes).

Intrigue, Rivet, Satisfy, AKA IRS.

First, you want to arouse curiosity on why you created the group in the first place. When people look at your group or even attend your event, you want them to ask you why you created this group in the first place.

Second, once that happens, pick a fascinating, true background story and leave out all the boring stuff so that it is engaging and leaves an impression on the person asking the question.

Third, after discussing your story, end with what you hope to accomplish personally and what you are trying to get out of the group you created yourself. Make sure it is accurate, and also paint the future in which they want to get what you want out of it.

For example, in in-person interactions, I tell people the following (paraphrased as it is different wording every time): I wanted a place where it is not just about work that surrounds the endless hustle and bustle. At the same time, I didn't want to do anything I tried so hard to achieve in my Korean language ability. By creating this Meetup, I hope to meet new people outside of my industry (tech) to learn and grow from people from other walks of life while preserving and enhancing the investment I have made in my Korean language ability.

That statement will invariably create a few scenarios depending on who I end up talking to: (1) meeting new friends—for people who are new in the area and (2) improving their Korean, which is hard to do while living in America. Because they see that I am invested in this personally, they also believe that by staying with the group, they will invariably receive the same result.

My current about page as of writing this book:

What we are about

In July 2022, I created this group to help Korean and English speakers talk and learn from each other across all levels. I aimed to create a close-knit group similar to the one I had in LA. As of now (April 2023), we have grown to 300+, with additional organizers volunteering their time. There are a few things I want to clarify and maintain as the purpose of the group. We do not want to die for the group's culture as we grow.

Goal:

Using language to make lifelong friends.

Guidelines:

- *Emotional safety*
- *Make genuine connections*
- *Walk away with at least a friend that makes you feel at home.*

Because of the group size, there will be some process changes to keep the events smoother and reduce the toll on the organizers as our group has grown significantly. If people are unaware, organizers must also pay money to Meetup.com to keep the group running and volunteering their time. Starting August 1, 2023, please review the process changes on the message board.

TL;DR: We will no longer make an attendee list on a first-come basis but based on multiple factors, such as members' activity within the group. Here is the list of Paid Patrons.

If people are unaware, Meetup charges the organizer a monthly fee to run the Meetup. Optional membership fees collected will be used to pay the monthly Meetup fees charged by Meetup.com.

For those looking for resources to improve your Korean based on your preferences, click here.

Selecting the Right Category and Keywords

Navigating Categories

Countless keywords and categories are available, so you must choose the one that aligns seamlessly with your group's focus. That will be easier for others to search through. Uncover strategies to stand out within your desired category, ensuring your community is visible and appealing to those with similar interests.

Pick all the categories under your primary and related content for this one. Picking categories can be important because it helps the group target the right users who are searching. For example, I listed anything that would make people want to learn Korean, such as Korean dramas, K-pop, etc. For others, getting a job in tech would involve programming, program management, LeetCode, etc.

I would put less emphasis on this as your goal is to make your first series of events as fantastic as possible so that it becomes a word of mouth instead of strictly relying on Meetup.com to advertise randomly for the new attendees. Frankly, there will come to a point where you hope it stops sending you new members.

Strategic Use of Keywords

Unlock the power of keywords to boost your group's discoverability. We will explore tools and methods to identify keywords relevant to your community, empowering you to strategically integrate them into your group's description and increase your group's visibility.

You can use several tools to see what most people search for and include those in the group descriptions. You can use ChatGPT or other AI tools nowadays to generate several of the most searched keywords on the web and use various social media platforms to see what people searched the most. I also use Headline's Coschedule AI generator to see what heading and tagline people will most resonate with to generate ideas I would want in my group's description. This phase is only essential in the early stage of the group creation; as the group goes on, this part will become less and less important going forward.

Choosing an Attractive Group Name and Logo

Naming Your Community

Your group's name is its calling card. This section guides you through selecting a memorable and resonant name. Real-world examples illustrate effective naming strategies, helping you balance creativity, clarity, and relevance.

I called my group "Korean Language Group Bay Area." Think of it as a tagline. I would use tools like Headline Analyzer from Coschedule to have AI develop different interesting taglines you prefer. However, it is essential to highlight the purpose where many flowery words do not directly tell users what the group is about. In my case, the focus is on the Korean language, and the location is in the Bay Area.

However, looking back, it could now be better given a better experience. I could have chosen "Korean-English Language Group in SF Bay Area" as it better depicts the group's intention. I believe I got lucky by not stating "English" or "SF" in my area, mainly because we are in the USA, so the English component is indirectly inferred.

Also, the Bay Area is renowned for its location in the USA. It is near Silicon Valley, so the location was also easily understood. I lucked out, but whatever name you choose has to answer two questions: (1) How can they grow from joining your group, and (2) Where is it so they can see if they can access it from their dwelling?

Crafting a Distinctive Picture

A picture is the visual emblem of your community, so familiarize yourself with the principles of practical visual appeal. Given it is a community, and as mentioned, you want to have some social proof established or, rather, as much social proof as you can generate. For professionally tailored groups, you want power-hitters in your industry that you have in the events that people can recognize.

For example, if you have a career club, you can show pictures of famous CEOs in your photographs that attended your event. Other social events, such as mine, involve practicing the language; you want to show many people and Koreans in the group. Also, since it is also a social group, and people are generally drawn to attractive visuals, it would be great to have at least one or two good-looking people in the picture. Although this sounds harsh, when you look through various catalogs, you are more drawn to better-looking people when making purchases. The same can be said of attracting newcomers to your group. Frankly, although imperfect, that is one of the main reasons I have kept my profile picture the same from ten to twenty years ago. Back then, I was a student, and girls were hitting on me and handing me their phone numbers without me asking, so I decided to keep that up to attract more members to the group.

Setting Up Your Page Effectively

Crafting a Compelling About Section

Your page serves as your group's virtual home. Explore the components of a compelling About section, putting together your mission, themes, and activities into a narrative that engages potential members.

In this section, take everything you did in the previous chapter and combine it here. For reference on my current about page, repasting here:

Goal:

Using language to make lifelong friends.

Guidelines:

- *Emotional safety*

- *Make genuine connections*

- *Walk away with at least a friend that makes you feel at home.*

Because of the group size, there will be some process changes to keep the events smoother and reduce the toll on the organizers as our group has grown significantly. If people are unaware, organizers must also pay money to Meetup.com to keep the group running and volunteering their time. Starting August 1, 2023, please review the process changes on the message board.

TL;DR: We will no longer make an attendee list on a first-come basis but based on multiple factors, such as members' activity within the group. Here is the list of Paid Patrons.

If people are unaware, Meetup charges the organizer a monthly fee to run the Meetup. Optional membership fees collected will be used to pay the monthly Meetup fees charged by Meetup.com.

For those looking for resources to improve your Korean based on your preferences, click here.

Utilizing Platform Features

Unlock the full potential of features to enhance your group's functionality. I used Meetup.com as a guide for creating groups. Here is how to use those tools effectively.

- **Title**: Whatever title you start with, keep things consistent. I have the following in my Meetup example: 12/16 MeetUp in Mountain View. The location always follows the dates.

- **Date and Time**: I recommend starting at the same time and on the same day of the week, for example, Saturday from 3:00 to 5:00 PM.

- **Duration**: I highly recommend at least one hour, as people will trickle in late. Anything under one hour is not recommended. Depending on your preference, recommend two hours to start and then adjust down or up. D

- **Feature photo**: When you upload the image, check the dimensions to ensure the picture shows up correctly or as expected. It is best if the featured photo is different for every event to create freshness unless it is a repeat of a similar event in the past, such as the exact location or type of event, to build familiarity.

- **Description**: I recommend what is stated in the suggestion by Meetup with additional helpful hints. Show additional context on how to find the group explicitly, such as a banner sign or colored clothing. Also, please include suggested parking information for those who drive to minimize delays.

- **Topics**: This is the area in which I am afraid I have to disagree with Meetup. Although you might want traffic and members, what is far more critical is highly engaged members. If you look at my tag, it differs from Meetup's suggestion. I would rather have engaging members than members that take up space. Of course, you can choose how best to grow your community.

- **Location**: I recommend not doing hybrid events. I suggest only doing in-person or online events. It is hard to create the same experience for both, and you are essentially doubling or even tripling the mental bandwidth for hybrids. Collecting feedback to ensure how to apply it best will also be more straightforward. Otherwise, you must determine whether the input belongs online or in person. I highly do not recommend hybrid events when first starting.

- **COVID-19 Safety Measures**: I usually leave this section blank...as we are well past the COVID-19 scare.

- **Event Fee**: I recommend having a free event and directing them to an external website for the paid event rather than tracking it on the app, as the app does not have the best payment feature.

- **Please Choose at Least One Communication Tool**: I recommend enabling chat and comments. Sometimes, you only want to communicate with confirmed attendees instead of letting the entire public forum see the message. So always encourage to be safe.

- **Optional Settings**: I recommend ignoring this section when first starting out and only starting to worry about this once you begin facing issues such as an attendee size being too big, people wanting to bring guests, etc.

At the bottom of the screen, you will see two buttons called "Preview" and "Publish." I recommend clicking "Preview" first to check the layout before publishing.

The Blueprint for Launch

Let us give you a comprehensive blueprint to guide your journey to launch. The clarity of your mission, the resonance of your group's identity, and the effectiveness of your visual elements collectively form a foundation for a thriving community. The following sections will delve into the practicalities of bringing this blueprint to life.

Preparing for Launch

The excitement builds as your vision takes shape, making it a little battle of nerves with all the stress to meet your expectations. Therefore, we will explore practical strategies for hosting engaging events, fostering community engagement, and ensuring a seamless launch. Your community is on the cusp of becoming a vibrant reality—stay tuned as we navigate the final steps toward launch.

Crafting Your Inaugural Event

The inaugural event sets the tone for your group's journey. From choosing the right venue to planning engaging activities, every detail contributes to a successful launch that captivates and retains your founding members.

The front marketing is done by effectively following the Setting Up Your Page section. When choosing the right venue, I encourage you to first focus on yourself and the type of venues that people similar to you would like. Earlier in the book, we did the Niche and Differentiation section exercise. What do most people prefer the avenue to be? Also, what is your style? The goal is to make sure the environment you pick will give you energy. At the same time, setting up the meeting should also provide you with energy.

For example, I get energy when surrounded by a background of people in a nice ambiance, so I picked cafes instead of parks for my venue. At the same time, people have told me that I enjoy controlled chaos. That means I like to go with the flow rather than have a set agenda that we have to accomplish. Because of that, I usually only set up the environment, and then once the people arrive, I decide the activity based on the vibe I am getting from the individuals and the group. If that stresses you out, you can check out the venue to ensure enough space, put up an agenda, and create a name tag, among other things. I would not say I like wearing nametags because I find them unfashionable even though they are functional, so you would never see me bringing nametags to the event as I would.

As a result, you need to find a venue that brings you the energy you need and figure out the style you prefer that naturally brings out your happy moments instead of adding stress to your events. In other books or recommendations, where they have a checklist, I would focus on the energy that you bring to the event as the prime way to keep people engaged. People can feel vibes from others, and creating an environment where others feel safe is more important than having the fanciest event from my perspective.

Managing Expectations: Your Role as a Leader

Leadership is critical to the success of any community group. This section explores the responsibilities and expectations associated with being a community leader. From facilitating discussions to managing conflicts, your role extends beyond event planning—it's about nurturing a supportive and inclusive community.

As mentioned in the previous section, managing the group's energy during the first few events is very important. As the leader or host of the event, you need to do a few things.

Facilitation

1. Please introduce yourself to everyone and ask about their motivation for joining the group. They will ask you why you are hosting or creating the group. We can then reference the

section where we mentioned the framework: Intrigue, Rivet, Satisfy, AKA IRS.

2. Introduce late members to members who arrived earlier to help them integrate into the social circle.

3. Break it into smaller groups if the group gets too big.

Managing Conflicts:

1. Always speak calmly when there is a conflict between members or the venue's manager.

2. Never raise your voice.

3. Always aim to find a win-win situation.

4. Comfortable disappointing one party if irreconcilable differences exist.

In one example, the venue manager was upset with us. While the members were upset, I offered to leave the venue or stay to address his concerns. Throughout the process, I was completely okay with walking away instead of demanding anyone to adhere to what I believed to be correct. Because he saw that I was firm on the choices, he moved us to a better location and successfully resolved the conflict.

Leveraging Social Media and External Promotion

Leverage social media and external promotion to extend your group's reach. This section provides a roadmap for utilizing platforms like Facebook, Twitter, and Instagram to complement your group's presence. Strategic external promotion can attract a broader audience and amplify your community's impact.

My advice is to only use one as opposed to using all. When first starting, using one platform like Meetup is enough to generate interest—using Meetup itself to display product market fit. There was another Meetup I began regarding the PM group meeting professionally. People are always either late or no-show. I closed the group shortly after (after one to two months). It is only possible to populate using external promotion if you have some traction with a small group and want to make the group bigger. Social media is leverage, but only if the seed is good. If the original content could be better, no matter how good your social media reach is, it will be a lot of wasted effort.

Once you have established the group you created, it will attract people who come regularly. I would choose the demographic of the group you want to attract.

Facebook: 74% of adult women are Facebook users, compared with 62% of all adult men. Platforms, which are all social media, are more popular with younger adults. Roughly 80% of 18–49-year-olds have an account. But older Americans are still represented. In the 50–64 age group, 65% are on Facebook, and 41% are 65 and older. [1]

Twitter or X: In the 18–24 age group, 45% report they use X. This compares to 33% for the 25–29 age group, 27% for the 30–49 age group, and 19% for the 50–64 age group. [2]

Instagram: The photo and video-sharing social network is top-rated among 18–24-year-olds. In this age group, 71% say they have an Instagram account. Usage drops off significantly for older Americans. In the 25–29 age group, just 54% have an account. Only 40% of Americans in the 30–49 age group report using Instagram, and the figure is 21% for those 50–64 years old. [3]

---

1   Aaron Smith and Monica Anderson, "Appendix A: Detailed Table," Pew Research Center: Internet, Science & Tech (Pew Research Center: Internet, Science & Tech, March 2018), https://www.pewresearch.org/internet/2018/03/01/social-media-use-2018-appendix-a-detailed-table/.

2   Aaron Smith and Monica Anderson, "Appendix A: Detailed Table," Pew Research Center: Internet, Science & Tech (Pew Research Center: Internet, Science & Tech, March 2018), https://www.pewresearch.org/internet/2018/03/01/social-media-use-2018-appendix-a-detailed-table/.

3   Hrishikesh Roy, "Twitter vs. Facebook vs. Instagram: Who Is Good to Target Audience?," www.linkedin.com, December 29, 2017, https://www.linkedin.com/pulse/twitter-vs-facebook-instagram-who-good-target-audience-hrishikesh-roy/.

Member Onboarding: Creating a Welcoming Environment

The first interactions members have with your group are crucial. This section outlines effective member onboarding strategies to create a welcoming environment. From personalized welcome messages to establishing community guidelines, your efforts in the onboarding process shape the members' experience and lay the foundation for a positive community culture.

Before the meeting, please set up a welcome message for each member joining your group to tell them two things. (1) Confirmation that they have joined the group and (2) Share your excitement about meeting them for the first time.

The Auto messages can be set up on various platforms. Kakao and Meetup.com both have those functionalities, for example. Instead of posting the directions here, it is better to go to their websites and determine the current process, as it might need to be updated here.

Also, when members come, it is best to have multiple founders with various strengths to help guide the environment. I usually categorize people into four main categories:

1. The Spontaneous One: able to develop different ideas in multiple events

2. People Person: loves people and gets along with everyone

3. Master Scheduler: shuffling events and activities from one place to another, keeping events and activities on schedule

4. Implementer: This person knows how to create the moving logistics and is detail-oriented, ensuring all the details are done correctly.

It is best if you have four of these individuals in your group. Otherwise, try to be the number two person. As a host, you must be prepared to talk to everyone who comes your way; if you can not, find someone to help so everyone feels welcome.

After your group starts, try to have all four lead the group. In my case, I only have three of the four after a year, so there is no need to rush to get all four as soon as possible.

Timing, mental, and within still operate on a last-minute basis. That means we don't have a number three individual in our group and can continue growing. Not having certain people within a group does not mean the group will fail.

Reflections on Your Journey Thus Far

Before launching, take a moment to reflect on your journey. This section guides you in assessing your group's readiness for launch, evaluating your goals, and making necessary adjustments. A reflective approach ensures you enter the launch phase with confidence and a clear vision for the future.

It would be best to evaluate using the Five W and H framework: Who, What, Where, When, Why, and How.

- Who: have you identified the type of individuals you want to cater to?

- What: Have you decided what type of niche or theme would make your group unique compared to others or what core fundamental areas you would want your group to anchor on?

- Where: Have you chosen the type of venue that you want your people to host?

- When: have you decided on the frequency and day of the week?

- Why: what motivates you to do this where you can easily articulate the reason so others will also want to go along with your "why?"

- How: have you decided how you will implement the event, whether through what social platforms you want to market them and the logistics you plan to set up for a smooth event?

Summary

Creating a successful offline group requires meticulous planning and a clear vision. This chapter guided you through defining your group's purpose and goals, crafting a mission statement, and identifying core themes and interests. Doing so can attract like-minded individuals who resonate with your group's values. You learned how to craft a compelling group description, select the right category and keywords for visibility, and choose an attractive group name and logo. The chapter also covers setting up an effective group page and leveraging platform features for optimal engagement. As you prepare for the launch, you will gain insights into organizing your inaugural event, managing your role as a leader, and utilizing social media for external promotion. Finally, the chapter emphasized the importance of a thoughtful onboarding process to create a welcoming environment for new members, ensuring a solid foundation for your community.

CHAPTER FOUR

Strategies for Successful Groups

Welcome to the core of community building—strategizing and executing successful groups. This chapter will delve into the intricacies of event planning, exploring strategies that transform gatherings into memorable experiences for your members. We will cover everything from deciding activities to managing logistics and handling issues. By the end of this chapter, you will have a comprehensive toolkit for planning and executing events that meet your group's objectives and foster a strong sense of community and connection among members.

Defining Your Event Strategy

Understanding Your Community's Preferences

A successful group begins with profoundly understanding your community. Explore methods for gathering insights into your members' preferences, interests, and availability. By aligning events with your community's desires, you will increase engagement and attendance.

There are two main ways to do this: (1) Find out along the way, (2) Do formal surveys and review feedback forms.

1. Find Out Along the Way

At each event, gauge everyone's interest and what they want more of. In the beginning, it is easy as you can talk to everyone who came through and ask them what brings them here, and then, in the end, ask for feedback on what they prefer doing in the next series of events. However, as the group gets larger, it becomes harder and harder to keep them together and get feedback individually because the input can be varied, and only some members show up each time. That means the input might only be relevant then, and the next time they show the input, it can be 180 degrees, as they could be attending a month or two from now.

2. Formal Surveys and Feedback Analysis

You can also send the survey monthly, quarterly, or at other frequencies. It is easy to reach almost all your members, but the issue with the response rate is generally low. If you get a 5% response rate, it is good.

Also, use Meetup.com, as I mentioned. Meetup.com will send regular feedback to your members after they attend the event. You can then browse through the comments section to see what they liked and did not like about your event and improve upon them. The problem is that most comments differ from what you are looking for because you needed to create the questions yourself. So, you can only get the answers you want to know if you need to ask the specific questions you want to ask to get more feedback.

Diversifying Event Types

Variety is the spice of community life. Learn how to diversify your event offerings to cater to different interests and preferences within your community. Discover the various event types that resonate with your members, from casual socials to specialized workshops.

One of the pitfalls I have noticed in running events that eventually disbanded is the need for more variety. Either you build variety within the event's environment, or you have to develop new activities for the event. If the event and location are always the same and everything is set up with only the convenience of the organizer in mind, attendees will get bored over time. It is easier to grow when there is novelty.

As a result, there are few examples of how to make the events enjoyable. The first thing I mentioned was to make it in the event environment. For me, that is what I did. I chose a different venue every single time the event took place. Given that we did not have more than five to ten people at a time when we first started, it was easy to find and jump around different cafes. It also served two purposes. The people were interested in the Korean language and the locations where they could find hidden gems they had never seen before. Just showing up is a novelty in itself. Second, given my style caters to the needs of the individuals who show up, it also means that unless the same people show up, the energy I create with the group will also be widely different each time. Given those two scenarios, the environment from the event location and changing the schedule on the fly based on the people attending create a novel experience for each person attending the event.

Another way to make the event enjoyable is to have various events. For example, one can be a casual meet-and-greet, then change to a workshop event, then a speaker event, then a one-on-one speed networking event, etc. By constantly having a variety of styles of events, people will find the novelty interesting and attend these events regularly as they will always be energized.

Crafting Memorable Event Experiences

Fostering Connection and Inclusivity

The essence of a successful event lies in fostering genuine connections. Explore strategies to create inclusive environments where every member feels welcome. Discover ways to nurture a sense of belonging, from icebreaker activities to mindful event design.

Social groups are more accessible, but professional groups will invariably be more difficult. People often attend events to get something out of it, so it can be very transactional if someone goes, gets something out of it, and disappears completely. Unfortunately, if the event is built upon a transactional connection, it can disappear anytime without warning.

Instead, attempt to get to know each person and treat them as long-lost friends. A lot of the dating advice applies here. One of the main reasons why some guys who cold approach women are better than others, even if they say the same thing, is the frame they set from the moment the women notice them to when they open their mouths. The exact words come out differently when they project an air of comfort and confidence that they are best buddies. Similarly, creating a feeling of comfort and confidence when meeting someone new is more arduous to reject, especially in these platonic situations.

Balancing Structure and Flexibility

Finding the right balance between structured activities and free-flowing interactions is an art. This section guides you in tailoring your event format to your community's preferences, ensuring a harmonious blend of planned activities and organic connections.

Define the Purpose and Scope

The first step to creating a balanced meeting agenda is to define the purpose and scope of the event. Why are you meeting? What are the expected outcomes? Who are the participants? How long will the meeting last? These questions help you clarify the goals and boundaries of the event and avoid wasting time on irrelevant or tangential topics. You can also use the purpose and scope to prioritize the most critical and urgent items for the event and leave some room for flexibility in case of unforeseen events.

Use a Standard Format

A standard format can help you structure your events to be easy to follow and understand. A standard format typically includes the following elements: a location, a date and time, a list of planned interactions, and a closing remark. Depending on the nature and context of the event, you can also add other components, such as ground rules, pre-work, or feedback mechanisms. A standard format can help you organize your thoughts, communicate your expectations, and facilitate the flow of the event.

Be Realistic and Flexible

A realistic and flexible event can adapt to the reality and dynamics of the event. A realistic event guide considers the participants' available time, resources, and attention span. It does not overestimate or underestimate what can be achieved in the event. A flexible event allows adjustments, modifications, or deviations from the original plan based on the participant's real-time feedback, input, or needs. To be realistic and flexible, you need to monitor the progress and mood of the event and be ready to make changes if necessary. For example, if you find that people need to have deep conversations with each other, break them up into smaller groups. Or, if you find that your space is underutilized, create an icebreaker to utilize the real estate you have fully.

Use Facilitation Techniques

Facilitation techniques are methods or tools that can help you guide, engage, and manage the participants and the content of the meeting. Facilitation techniques help you balance the structure and flexibility of the meeting agenda by providing direction, clarity, and variety. For example, you can use facilitation techniques such as icebreakers, brainstorming, voting, or breakout sessions to warm up, generate ideas, make decisions, or divide tasks. You can also use facilitation techniques such as parking lot, check-in, or wrap-up to address questions, issues, or feedback that are not directly related to the agenda topics but are still necessary or relevant.

Seek Feedback and Improvement

The last tip to balance the structure and flexibility of the event is to seek feedback and improvement. Feedback can help you evaluate the effectiveness and efficiency of the meeting agenda and identify the strengths and weaknesses of your planning and facilitation skills. Improvement can help you learn from your experience and apply the lessons and best practices to future meetings. You can seek feedback and improvement by asking the participants for their opinions, suggestions, or ratings during or after the meeting. With applications like Meetup, you can peruse the ratings and feedback that Meetup automatically collects for you.

Practical Event Planning Tips

Creating a Seamless RSVP and Check-in Process

A smooth RSVP and check-in process sets the tone for a well-organized event. Explore practical tips for streamlining these processes, making it easy for members to participate, and minimizing logistical challenges.

The software will automatically allow people to register for the event. You can use many free event and group software, such as Facebook groups. Alternatively, you can pay more, like Meetup.com, about $25 a month (2024 price), to create a group and have the software to manage them. Regarding RSVP, ensure some allow you to have participants unreserved or reserve their attendance easily.

You are to mark off a list of attendees for the actual event. For small events, you can match the faces or ask them for their names to check off their names. However, for a big event, it is best to have a check-in counter so that people can easily find the check-in table and mark themselves as present.

Venue Selection and Logistics

Choosing the right venue is a crucial aspect of event planning. Additionally, remember logistics, such as seating arrangements, signage, and accessibility, to ensure a seamless experience.

To start, do not try to boil the ocean. Only when you have members who need special accommodations, do you begin to create them. Why optimize for one member when ninety-nine members don't need it? The return on effort is just not worth it. Instead, optimize for average attendees like you. After all, you are building the community because you are passionate about it. You want to get people as eager as you to attend the event. Pick places you wish to attend, whether that is the seating arrangement you would like or the specific signage that makes it easy to find.

For example, I enjoy visiting cafes, and their ambiance is essential to Mike. I want to experience the unique atmospheres of different cafes, so even if an event turns out to be disappointing, I still have a great time. This approach has been helpful; for instance, there was an event with low attendance, but I could enjoy the cafe before it closed.

Leveraging Sponsors and Partnerships

Strategic partnerships can enhance the quality and reach of your events. Explore ways to identify potential sponsors and partners and collaborate for mutual benefit. Successful alliances can bring added value to your community and elevate the overall event experience.

Partnership is an area that I have little experience in and have yet to achieve much success in. I recommend perusing other resources. I share my experience thus far: because of the group size, it became more accessible for people to market to my members. When I first decided to reach out to my potential sponsors, they were eager. However, the issue is that most of these products require payments. After all, sponsors want a positive return on their investment. Given that most of the products I pursued require certain payments that individuals can make themselves, the savings are not significant enough for people to be willing to spend. Also, because my initial Meetup started in the Bay Area, where software engineers dominate the landscape, people are less willing to spend money to save time.

In the Bay Area, most people have financial capital, but they hoard it. However, most of them are still very big on sales. Their most significant expenses are investing and paying for their kid's education. They are also good at optimizing expenses, so it has to bring value continually. The tradeoff from this group is that they never tend to get the best stuff because the best stuff is usually a premium and not the best value. As a result, to cater to my members in this category, I have to ensure they will have the most optimized value of things they cannot get themselves, no matter how much finessing they do.

Unfortunately, I cannot provide much from personal experience. Still, I have seen success with other groups who have done it quite successfully. I recommend reaching out to groups with a comprehensive sponsor list to get additional ideas on whether monetization is a huge deal for you.

Member Engagement Strategies

Pre-Event Engagement

Engaging members before the event builds anticipation and connection. Explore methods for pre-event engagement, including discussions, polls, and teaser content. Creating a buzz leading up to the event enhances member excitement and participation.

There are various ways to engage your attendees. For instance, one of the founding organizers of our group used an interesting approach. She would go on Tinder and match with multiple guys, invite all of them to the Korean language event, and bring them over. It brought a lot of excitement.

Another way is to send pre-event emails. You can send emails at set intervals before the event to remind attendees and help them prepare. Some apps, like Meetup.com, do this for you automatically before the event, so you do not have to worry about it.

Third, you can create a group chat for every person who signed up. In this big group chat, you can post announcements about the event that help members stay informed about the latest event updates. This helps spread the word very nicely.

During-Event Interaction

Maximizing member interaction during events contributes to a vibrant community experience. Learn strategies for facilitating conversations, networking, and group activities that encourage members to engage actively and form meaningful connections.

The best way to create lifelong engaged members is to have a best friend in the group. Think about any social group that you end up going to. Usually, it is because you like the group. Still, more importantly, you are now friends with someone, and you guys do a lot of stuff together, which makes things very interesting. From that perspective, you aim to see who will get along the best and, ideally, put them together.

Frankly, people naturally gravitate to those who are similar. One notable factor is that the new members sit with the new members, and the old members sit with the old ones. As a facilitator, it is your job to help them break down the barrier so both groups can mix and interact with each other. If you are passive, you will start to create small cohorts of groups. That is okay when it gets big enough, but you do not want it to be like that from the very beginning.

Post-Event Follow-Up

Remember, the event is ongoing when members leave the venue. Post-event engagement is equally vital. This section guides you in crafting effective post-event follow-up strategies, such as event recaps, member surveys, and ongoing discussions, to maintain momentum and foster lasting connections.

It is best to get feedback on the events ASAP. Various groups like Meetup.com send out feedback emails directly to your attendees. It helps you understand what is good and what is not so you can improve things in the future. Ideally, if you have events from week to week, it is excellent to keep the momentum going. Where minimum interactions online are necessary, it is best to maintain some form of messaging to ensure members stay engaged throughout the process.

Evaluating Event Success and Gathering Feedback

Setting Metrics and Goals

Define success for your groups by setting clear metrics and goals. Whether it is attendance numbers, member satisfaction, or community growth, establishing measurable objectives allows you to assess the impact of your events and make informed decisions.

I did not personally do this, but in hindsight, it is essential. Because I have been seeing regulars and that member growth has been steadily growing, I was not concerned about using metrics to track these things in any capacity. I can see the metrics in person with the attending members. However, to put things in practical terms, it is best to do the following to ensure your metrics are doing well.

1. Overall member growth rate

2. Overall repeat member attendance rate

Having those two already ensures you have the best way to measure the group's health and success. However, if you want more, you can do more, like measuring how long people stay, etc., to go deeper into those areas.

Gathering Constructive Feedback

Feedback is a valuable tool for improvement. Explore methods for collecting constructive feedback from your members, from surveys to open discussions. Utilize this feedback loop to refine your event strategies and continuously enhance the member experience.

Beyond getting feedback after every event, gathering input beyond the simple survey the app sends out or just cursory information is best. There are various ways to do this. Here are two examples:

1. Create a more in-depth study on what they hope to get from the event in a survey and tabularize the results into actionable items. Because the touch point is digital, the conversion rate is low. To increase responses, offer an incentive like drawing for a gift card to encourage more active participation.

2. Suppose the event has enough attendees, but it is small. In that case, you can ask them personally during the event to get feedback. The engagement rate is high, but gathering them will take time. See if you want to continue that process over time.

Navigating Challenges and Mitigating Risks

Handling Attendance Fluctuations

Attendance fluctuations are common at community events. Therefore, you should learn strategies for managing high and low attendance scenarios, ensuring your events remain engaging and successful regardless of the turnout.

There are various ways to start testing venues, event structures, and geo-locations to see which has the most individuals. Usually, similar people tend to live in similar geographical areas. Once you find the best match, stick with it. In my experience, the following occurs:

1. The Bay Area, within twenty minutes of K-town (since it is a Korean language Meetup), has the best number of turnouts.

2. Females usually have a higher turnout than males, so it is easy to draw guys to the Meetup, given that the event generally has more female members. The ratio started with 70% females and 30% males, and after about a year, it is about 50% male and 50% female.

3. Small event structures attract particular members, and large event structures attract different sets. All those events will allow members to be continually involved instead of losing old members when the group was small. Still, they fall off due to the increase in the size of the groups over time.

Addressing Conflicts and Disruptions

Community dynamics can sometimes lead to conflicts or disruptions. This section guides addressing and mitigating these challenges, fostering a positive and inclusive environment for all members.

Conflicts can arise from member disagreements or disagreements with the venue. Here is a simple framework and rules to remember when they happen.

1. Keep a neutral voice, and do not raise your voice.

2. Understand the root of the problem before deciding what to do.

3. Stay willing to be flexible.

Also, rules should be enforced if that is the only way to resolve things. Sometimes, these events are great things that help you establish policies and regulations to ensure a smooth process. If an event transpired due to the creation of the rules, however strict, the members will be more understanding than a blanket rule created because the organizer wants it. That also means it is easy to enforce the rules.

Another real-life example was when we indirectly disrespected the owner of the venue; because of that, he was very frustrated and had a somber tone. It created a horrible ambiance for all the members. He was referencing the top three items mentioned about keeping a neutral voice, understanding the root problem, and being willing to be flexible. In the entire interface, I did not raise my voice and asked questions about his frustrations. I could extract from his emotions that he was visibly upset because he wanted us to wait for him, and we did not listen to him multiple times and took matters into our own hands. From our perspective, we also fit in as we had been waiting for a long time and would not just stand there and stay forever. So instead of arguing with him why we did what we did, given his root of anger is the lack of respect for his ownership of the venue, I told him we would now respect his wishes and move everything back and also happy to leave the venue to outside if he chooses for our inconsideration.

Given that I had done nothing to his adverse reaction, he realized he might also be wrong. One of the first signs was the lower voice of the angry party. His voice started to go down, and he even offered another solution: move us to another place. I, maintaining the principle of being flexible, agreed to his request readily. We ended up with a better setup than before.

It is essential to understand that fighting fire with fire increases the fire. Finding the root of the issue and looking at it in the third person, like a drama, will help you maintain the three principles I laid out earlier.

Contingency Planning

Anticipate and prepare for unexpected challenges with effective contingency planning. From unforeseen weather changes to technical difficulties, contingency plans ensure your events can adapt and continue smoothly.

This Dating 101 is for men. When you make plans with a girl on a date, you usually have plans B and C in place. Otherwise, if plan A fails, the girl will think you are incompetent in the basics of human life, even though it is not your fault. Similarly, attendees who suffered logistic issues of no fault to the organizer or host will blame the organizer or host as incompetent. So, always have plans B and C in place when plan A goes awry.

Alternatively, you can pick a place that has various contingencies built in. For example, if you choose a plaza that has multiple cafes (if your primary place is a type of cafe), then you can easily have plans B and C right there by simply checking the other two to three places nearby within walking distance.

So, always have two to three plans before attending your event as a host.

Summary

As we conclude this section, you now possess a comprehensive blueprint for planning and executing successful groups. The following chapters will build upon this foundation, exploring advanced strategies, emerging trends, and innovative approaches to elevate your community-building journey further.

CHAPTER FIVE

Advanced Strategies for Event Excellence

As the event landscape evolves, so does the culture surrounding community engagement and participation. This chapter delves deeper into the emerging trends shaping event culture, from the rise of hybrid and virtual experiences to the use of advanced technology and specialized events. It offers valuable insights and strategies to help keep your group at the forefront of innovation. The COVID-19 pandemic has accelerated the adoption of dual events, leading to the simultaneous hosting of virtual and in-person gatherings. While online events offer accessibility and convenience, in-person events foster deeper connections. Hybrid events, though challenging, present unique opportunities for engagement. This section will explore these dynamics, the effective use of technology, the importance of specialized events for niche communities, and strategies for building sustainable and inclusive groups. By harnessing these trends, organizers can create vibrant, resilient communities that thrive in the ever-changing event landscape.

Exploring Emerging Trends in Event Culture

As the event landscape evolves, so do the community culture trends. This section explores emerging trends, from hybrid events to virtual experiences, providing insights and strategies to keep your group at the forefront of community innovation.

Due to COVID, many events try to accommodate dual events by simultaneously having virtual and in-person events and a hybrid of in-person and online events. I would rank the difficulty in the following manner:

1. Online

2. Offline

3. Hybrid

Online events are accessible because everyone can do them in the comfort of their own home. As long as you are in the same time zone, you can even expand your reach to other cities within a few hours of your time zone. This approach is perfect for introverts and Gen Z who do not like social interactions. Some people make lifelong friends through virtual meetings, such as gaming.

However, it is easier to build a connection because you can see that person holistically from their body language. As a result, if there is enough good traction, then the engagement level of repeat members will be higher.

Hybrids are the hardest because the organizers and hosts need to simultaneously ensure two separate experiences and converge them into one, making them three distinct experiences. However, the more complicated something is, the better the opportunity for you. If you can nail something this hard, it will be hard for others not to take you seriously going forward, and you will have a unique community that others can't easily emulate.

Harnessing Technology for Enhanced Group

Technology can be a powerful ally in creating a dynamic and interactive group. Explore ways to leverage tools and platforms, from event management software to virtual reality, to enhance the overall event experience and engage members in new and exciting ways.

I do two things with mine. Many software programs have tools for managing members. For example, Meetup.com has event management software for organizers. It helps me check people in and out as needed.

I also use Grammarly and ChatGPT for email announcements, which I use to correct my grammar because I want to type without worrying about how it sounds and let AI help me. For ChatGPT, I have drafted an announcement template so I do not have to think too hard about what to write and only correct and enhance the existing messages.

These things alone save me tens of hours when doing the offline community.

Crafting Specialized Events for Niche Communities

Specialized events tailored to specific niches can deepen member engagement and attract a dedicated audience. Learn how to identify opportunities for specialized events within your community and explore strategies for planning and executing these unique gatherings.

In the Meetup, I created many Korean-related events, such as New Year's parties, K-pop events, and other K-drama-related interactions. Some explorations include going to a Korean festival or hosting K-drama movie nights. These more specialized events help bring the members together. Luckily, I am also grateful for members who host free Korean language classes that bring the members closer together.

The specialized events would have to be different for another Meetup. For example, crypto Meetups might be bitcoin exchange parties or new coin whitepaper reviews.

Building a Sustainable and Inclusive Community

Sustainability and inclusivity are pillars of a thriving community. This section guides creating a sustainable model that ensures the longevity of your group. Explore strategies for fostering inclusivity, diversity, and a sense of belonging within your community.

One of the most important things to consider when running a group is whether you will still do it in your free time. The reason is that once it becomes a part-time job, it becomes less exciting and feels like a chore, especially since the monetary compensation for running a group is nearly nonexistent. As a result, to avoid an unsustainable model, you should be inclusive with the members and your own time.

Once the members got to about 150 members, running the group started to feel like a job. The reason is that with constant members coming, finding a location is more precise, creating the event is also more accurate, and ensuring everyone has a good time is more energy-draining. Nowadays, when I host events, I almost get zero practice in my Korean because I am so busy hosting individual experiences. As a result, I had to change various systems and rules to ensure that I also benefitted and to keep it from becoming a part-time job.

In my example, I started allocating time to the group. If the time exceeded the allocated time, I quit my activity for the month. Similarly, you need to ensure that the size of the events allows you to be engaged. Still, the quality of your events is maintained. Anything over fifteen people will take up most of my time for the month and start feeling like a part-time job. As a result, I now keep the individuals around ten to twenty people to avoid myself from burning out or having very little energy to give to the members.

For you, it would be best to balance your interests with the community to avoid burnout.

Advanced Member Engagement Strategies

Deepen member engagement with basic and advanced strategies. Discover innovative approaches to connecting members and nurturing a dynamic and creative community ecosystem, from mentorship programs to collaborative projects.

One of the ways that occurred for my group was creating small silo groups as the group got bigger so they could get to know each other more.

As of writing this book, I believe there are three smaller silo groups: Hiking, Korean Language, and Tennis. Those with regular cadence are best. It is as if everyone expects an event to occur and will continue to be involved, and those who need to know when it will appear tend to be less engaged. Because of the smaller size, the event usually needs to be held more often than the more prominent groups so that the event becomes part of their weekly or monthly routine.

The Art of Scaling: Growing Your Community

As your community flourishes, scaling becomes a strategic consideration. This section explores the art of scaling, offering insights into managing growth, maintaining community culture, and ensuring that your group continues to thrive as it expands.

When it grows, just like a startup, the culture is more challenging to maintain, and the process needs to be started to avoid complete chaos. Having spontaneous decisions with twenty members vs. 200 members is different. It is easy to accommodate everyone's needs when it is small versus trying to accommodate everyone's needs when the group is significant. You would need to make strategic tradeoffs that would likely piss some members off because of specific changes to preserve the culture of the group.

For example, with my Meetup, I wanted to ensure that everyone feels like they can make friends here and not feel alone within their community. To do that invariably means a more profound connection vs a shallow connection. As a result, my events can be manageable, or people will not have a deeper connection with them. Invariably, that means not everyone can come every week because of this. I also know that will result in me losing certain members who would like to come every week. One of the other avenues was to ensure those who wanted to come in put some skin in the game and also let me know they were more committed than those who tend to change their mind at the last minute.

I also now have a membership plan mainly used to cover the cost of hosting the Meetup, and it is priced accordingly based on the number of people I expect to sign up. With this, if these people sign up to come, I can be sure that they will come versus not showing up and canceling at the last minute. The worst thing for a host is to make a drastic change of plans at the last minute.

There is now also a process document that I expect people to read. It is similar to a rule book or company handbook that people should abide by if they want to be part of the community. If they don't read, and I enforce it, that is on them instead of on me. Some might not like it, but the behavior will go like this once enforced. Although harmful in the short-term, it will have longer beneficial expectations. Otherwise, one person's negative behavior will affect the group dynamic. The expression "One bad apple can spoil the bunch" rings true here.

The tradeoff is your community specific to see what type of culture you want to preserve and be willing to mitigate the negative effect of such decisions in the future.

Celebrating Milestones: Reflecting and Looking Forward

As your group achieves milestones, take a moment to reflect on the journey. At this stage, you must focus on three things:

- A framework for celebrating achievements.

- Expressing gratitude to your community.

- Setting new goals for the future.

Celebrate the milestones that mark the ongoing success of your group.

It is always good to express thanks and gratitude along the way. How you decide to do it is on your own, but here are some ways I express thanks along the way.

When the group was small, I would offer to buy coffee for everyone who came to the event. Some accepted it, while some rejected it. I would also thank the members because their contributions and involvement kept this group alive.

As the group grows, the number of volunteers also needs to increase. To address this, I thanked the proactive volunteers by picking a convenient date and treating those who could attend to lunch or coffee. Those who could not join usually understood, as they were already volunteering their time and tended to be more generous. These volunteers contrast with individuals who typically try to receive more than they give.

My next plan is that if there is a significant membership sign-up and a lot of money left over, I will organize a holiday party with those funds to give back to the paid members.

As a result, this will highly depend on your situation and how you want to give. Still, having a feeling of gratitude and gracefulness is essential.

Member-Led Initiatives and Empowerment

Empowering Members as Event Organizers

Empower your members to take the lead in organizing events. Learn how to foster a culture where members feel encouraged and supported to initiate and host their gatherings. Member-led initiatives contribute to the diversity and richness of your community's event offerings.

One way to encourage member contributions instead of just doing it out of their good heart is to incentivize the benefits they receive when hosting or leading. That way, they get priority access that others do not. For mine, they get two benefits: they get prioritized over the regular members when the event is complete, and they can decide who gets to attend among the open slots for regular members.

One of the best ways is to align that the more contributions one makes to the organization, the more benefit or privilege one gets. Otherwise, some might resent putting in more effort than what they are arriving for and that their labor is being exploited.

Other groups have free drink vouchers for hosts that can add up to $10-20 depending on which part of the city you are part of. As a result, there has to be some benefit that members will care about after being part of a community's leadership group.

Creating Membership Roles

When leadership responsibilities become too much, distribute them among committed members. Explore strategies for creating member committees or assigning specific roles within your community. Shared leadership ensures the sustainability and growth of your community over time.

As any community grows, it is essential that the leadership team also grows to enable scale. Because of that, there usually need to be different levels of admin privileges to ensure that the group goes smoothly. As the founder or the person who determines the group's culture, you must ensure that this person has no authority over other members. This person usually dictates the culture and is also the ultimate decision-maker when enforcing the rules.

Then, the levels are dependent on the size of your leadership team. I split it up into two layers. The first layer is the one that can create and host events, whereas the second layer can remove and assign new leadership at the first layer. I have two to distribute the workload and ensure that the second layer of leadership has the same cultural goal as me in facilitating the group. Most importantly, they must be liked or respected by the group. Otherwise, if their voices and opinions are respected, it would be easier for them to enforce many of the group's rules and policies.

I prefer a flat leadership committee to a nested one, mainly because decision-making becomes slower when there are too many layers in the organization. Some might like that, as it filters non-essential decisions at the lower level.

Summary

As we conclude this exploration of emerging trends in event culture, it is essential to highlight the importance of member-led initiatives. Empowering members to take on leadership roles fosters a more profound sense of trust and commitment within the group and provides individuals with a sense of responsibility and ownership. These initiatives enhance the diversity and richness of your community's events, ensuring sustained engagement and vitality. By embracing these trends and strategies, you keep your group at the forefront of innovation and cultivate a dynamic, inclusive, and resilient community. Lastly, remember that the collaboration within your group's efforts and shared leadership within your group for a thriving community paves the way for continued growth and success.

CHAPTER SIX

Hypothetical Case Studies

It is all a hazy dream until you practically set out to build a community. That is when it dawns on you that not only are you utterly inexperienced in creating a group but also new to anticipating its myriad needs and challenges. What people want, where I begin, what I should aim for, etc., all seem like impossible questions. Therefore, in this chapter, I will give you case studies that will emulate your possible experience as a new organizer and help you along the way. These are not real case studies but hypothetical scenarios I have seen played out in various events. You can use the case studies and the previously given knowledge in this book to delineate your steps and make your custom method for success. Let's go.

Case Study 1: "Nature Enthusiasts Unite"

Background

Meetup Group: Nature Lovers Community

Organizer: Sarah Thompson

Location: Denver, Colorado

An avid nature enthusiast, Sarah Thompson established the Nature Lovers Community in Denver, Colorado. The group aimed to connect individuals passionate about the outdoors, from hiking and birdwatching to conservation efforts.

Challenges Faced

- Seasonal Challenges: Denver's climate posed seasonal challenges, with winter weather limiting outdoor activities.

- Limited Initial Membership: The group struggled to attract members initially, facing competition from established nature groups.

Strategies Implemented

- Diverse Event Calendar: Sarah diversified the event calendar to include indoor nature-related activities during the winter months, such as nature-themed workshops and guest speaker events.

- Collaborations with Existing Groups: Sarah initiated collaborations with other nature-focused Meetup groups, fostering cross-promotion and mutual support.

Potential Outcomes

- Year-Round Engagement: The diverse event calendar resulted in year-round engagement, attracting members even during winter.

- Community Growth: Collaborations increased the group's visibility, leading to a steady influx of new members.

Case Study 2: "Tech Innovators Collective"

Background

Meetup Group: Tech Innovators Collective

Organizer: Raj Patel

Location: Silicon Valley, California

Raj Patel founded the Tech Innovators Collective, a group dedicated to fostering collaboration among tech enthusiasts, entrepreneurs, and industry professionals in Silicon Valley.

Challenges Faced

- High Member Turnover: Silicon Valley's dynamic environment led to high turnover as members frequently changed jobs or relocated.

- Balancing Skill Levels: The group comprised members with varying technical expertise, making it challenging to plan events suitable for everyone.

Strategies Implemented

- Professional Development Workshops: Raj introduced workshops focused on skill development, providing value to members regardless of job changes.

- Skill-Level Segmented Events: Events were categorized based on skill levels, ensuring both beginners and experts found relevant opportunities for learning and networking.

Potential Outcomes

- Increased Member Retention: Professional development workshops contributed to member retention, as individuals saw the group as a valuable resource beyond networking.

- Diverse Event Offerings: Skill-level segmented events appealed to a broader audience, attracting both seasoned professionals and those entering the tech industry.

Case Study 3: "Creative Minds Artistry"

Background

Meetup Group: Creative Minds Artistry

Organizer: Jasmine Williams

Location: New York City, New York

Jasmine Williams established Creative Minds Artistry to unite New York City artists, writers, and creatives for collaborative projects and networking opportunities.

Challenges Faced

- Competing Cultural Scene: New York City's vibrant cultural scene posed challenges in standing out and attracting artists.

- Diverse Creative Disciplines: The group comprised individuals with diverse creative backgrounds, making it challenging to create events that appealed to everyone.

Strategies Implemented

- Unique Collaborative Projects: Jasmine initiated unique collaborative art projects that showcased the diverse talents within the group.

- Discipline-Specific Events: Events were organized based on creative disciplines (e.g., visual arts, writing) to address diverse disciplines, allowing members to choose events aligned with their interests.

Potential Outcomes

- Increased Visibility: Unique collaborative projects garnered attention and expanded the group's visibility within the broader artistic community.

- Discipline-Focused Engagement: Discipline-specific events increased engagement, as members found events tailored to their creative interests.

Case Study 4: "Global Nomads Connect"

Background

Meetup Group: Global Nomads Connect

Organizer: Alexei Ivanov

Location: Remote/Online

Alexei Ivanov established Global Nomads Connect, a virtual community for individuals with a nomadic lifestyle. The group aimed to provide a supportive network for remote workers, digital nomads, and frequent travelers.

Challenges Faced

- Time Zone Variability: Coordinating events and engagement activities across different time zones presented logistical challenges.

- Maintaining Virtual Engagement: Sustaining meaningful connections in a virtual environment requires innovative approaches.

Strategies Implemented

- Time-Zone-Friendly Events: Alexei scheduled events at varying times to accommodate members from different regions, ensuring inclusivity.

- Interactive Virtual Platforms: The group utilized interactive platforms beyond Meetup, such as virtual reality spaces and collaboration tools, to enhance engagement.

Potential Outcomes

- Global Inclusivity: Time-zone-friendly events enabled members worldwide to participate, fostering a truly international community.

- Innovative Engagement: Exploring virtual platforms beyond Meetup enriched member engagement, providing unique and immersive experiences.

Reflection on Case Studies

Common Themes

Adaptability: Successful groups demonstrated remarkable adaptability, skillfully navigating challenges and meeting the evolving needs of their members. For instance, the Nature Lovers Community, organized by Sarah Thompson in Denver, can adapt to seasonal constraints by diversifying its event calendar to include indoor nature-themed activities during winter months. This flexibility ensured continuous member engagement despite harsh weather conditions. Similarly, Raj Patel's Tech Innovators Collective in Silicon Valley can address high member turnover by offering professional development workshops, making the group a valuable resource beyond mere networking.

Innovation: Innovative strategies were central to these groups' success, driving both event planning and community engagement. In New York City, Jasmine Williams of Creative Minds Artistry can introduce unique collaborative art projects to increase the group's visibility and appeal. The Tech Innovators Collective can also implement skill-level segmented events, catering to both beginners and seasoned professionals, which broadens their appeal and attracts a diverse audience. Such creativity can resolve immediate issues and set these groups apart as leaders in their respective fields.

Community-Centric Approaches: Prioritizing community needs was a common thread in each case study, fostering a strong sense of belonging and creating significant value for members. Alexei Ivanov's Global Nomads Connect, for example, tackled the challenge of coordinating events across different time zones by scheduling time-zone-friendly events and using interactive virtual platforms. Virtual platforms ensured that members worldwide felt included and engaged. In the Nature Lovers Community, Sarah's collaborations with other nature-focused groups enhanced mutual support and cross-promotion, contributing to community growth and year-round engagement. By focusing on the well-being and interests of their members, these groups can build loyal, engaged communities that thrive.

Final Thoughts

As you turn the final pages of this guide, remember that you are part of a global community of catalysts. Meetup organizers bring people together, spark connections, and create spaces for shared experiences. Your role as a community builder is pivotal, and your efforts' impact extends far beyond your group's boundaries.

As we conclude our exploration of offline communities and group management, we must reflect on the journey we have taken together. Throughout this book, we have delved deep into the dynamics of offline gatherings, dissected successful community models, and outlined strategies for launching and nurturing thriving groups. Now, armed with knowledge and insights, it's time to distill our learnings into actionable takeaways.

First and foremost, we have uncovered the inherent paradox of the digital age: while technology has enabled unprecedented connectivity, it has also left many yearning for authentic human interaction. This longing for genuine connection catalyzes the rise of offline communities, providing individuals with a space to forge meaningful relationships beyond the confines of screens and algorithms.

Understanding the landscape of offline communities is paramount for anyone seeking to embark on this journey. From analyzing successful groups to crafting engaging pages and implementing best practices, laying a solid foundation is critical to creating a vibrant community space. By defining clear goals, crafting compelling descriptions, and leveraging social media for promotion, you can attract like-minded individuals and foster a sense of belonging from the outset.

Launching and managing an offline group requires careful planning and strategic execution. From defining your group's purpose to managing expectations as a leader, every step plays a crucial role in setting the stage for success. Member onboarding is equally essential, as creating a welcoming environment ensures that newcomers feel valued and embraced by the community.

As your group begins to flourish, you must employ strategies for continued growth and engagement. Crafting memorable event experiences, balancing structure with flexibility, and soliciting feedback are all integral components of a thriving community ecosystem. By embracing member-led initiatives and exploring emerging trends, you can cultivate a culture of empowerment and innovation within your group. Do not just rely on yourself; give everyone a chance to shine!

The case studies presented throughout this book, especially in the sixth chapter, offer valuable insights into potential examples of thriving offline communities. They gave you a blueprint to get started on your journey. By reflecting on these diverse experiences, you can glean inspiration and guidance for your trip.

In closing, building and nurturing offline communities is both rewarding and challenging. It requires dedication, empathy, and a genuine passion for fostering human connection. As you embark on this path, remember that every interaction, every event, and every member contributes to your community's rich tapestry. Embrace the journey, celebrate the milestones, and never underestimate the transformative power of offline connection. We can create spaces where individuals thrive, relationships flourish, and communities endure.